Aïda

AS TOLD BY

Leontyne Price

ILLUSTRATED BY

LEO AND DIANE DILLON

Based on the opera by Giuseppe Verdi

Gulliver Books

Harcourt Brace Jovanovich, Publishers

SAN DIEGO   NEW YORK   LONDON

Library of Congress Cataloging-in-Publication Data
Price, Leontyne
Aïda / as told by Leontyne Price and
illustrated by Leo and Diane Dillon. — 1st ed.
p.   cm.
"Gulliver books."
Summary: Retells the story of Verdi's opera
in which the love of the enslaved Ethiopian princess
for an Egyptian general brings tragedy
to all involved.
ISBN 0-15-200405-X
1. Verdi, Giuseppe, 1813–1901. Aïda — Juvenile literature.
[1. Verdi, Giuseppe, 1813–1901. Aïda.
2. Operas — Stories, plots, etc.]
I. Dillon, Leo, ill. II. Dillon, Diane, ill.
III. Verdi, Giuseppe, 1813–1901. Aïda. IV. Title.
ML3930.V4P7   1990
782.1'026'9' — dc20   89-36481

HBJ

First edition   A B C D E

The illustrations in this book were done in acrylics on acetate and marbleized paper.
The metal frame was designed and created by Lee Dillon.
Calligraphy by Dia Calhoun / Design 26
The text type was set in Trump Mediaeval by Thompson Type, San Diego, California.
Color separations were made by Bright Arts, Ltd., Singapore.
Printed and bound by Tien Wah Press, Singapore
Production supervision by Warren Wallerstein
Designed by Leo and Diane Dillon

To Mama, Daddy, and George with all my love
— L. Price

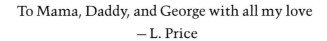

To Bonnie and Warren, our appreciation and admiration
— L. & D. Dillon

ong ago, in the faraway land of Ethiopia, there lived a Princess named Aïda. She was fair as the sunrise and gentle as starlight touching a flower. Her father, the great King Amonasro, loved her dearly.

It was a time of terrible fear and danger in Ethiopia, for the kingdom was at war with its neighbor, Egypt. Both countries raided each other's lands, killing or enslaving their enemies.

For the safety of his people, King Amonasro set strict boundaries at the borders of his country, and no Ethiopian was allowed beyond them.

The Princess Aïda was young and, locked within the palace, she grew restless. So, one morning, Aïda and her trusted friends disobeyed the King's command. They disguised themselves and slipped away from the palace guards.

It was a glorious day of freedom, out in the gentle breezes and lush green fields of their beautiful country. But Aïda wandered farther than she should have. Off on her own, enjoying the warm sun and fresh country air, she did not hear her friends in the distance when they shouted, "Aïda! Beware! Come back!"

Once again, Egyptian soldiers had invaded Ethiopia, crossing the south edge of the River Nile. Now they marched toward Aïda.

When she finally did hear her friends' warning, it was too late. Soldiers seized her. Bound with ropes and chains, Aïda, the Royal Princess of Ethiopia, was carried off to Egypt as a slave.

Aïda had learned her royal lessons well. She revealed to no one that she was the daughter of King Amonasro of Ethiopia. But her beauty and noble bearing attracted great attention. So sparkling and unusual was she that the all-powerful Pharaoh, the ruler of Egypt, chose her from among thousands of captured slaves to be his gift—a personal handmaiden—to his only daughter, the Princess Amneris.

It was easy for Aïda to perform the duties of a servant, for she remembered what her own handmaidens had done. The Egyptian Princess Amneris was fascinated, for Aïda was different from any slave she had ever seen. She wanted her new handmaiden to be her closest companion.

Even with the special privileges granted to one so close to the Royal Princess, Aïda felt nothing but despair. All her life she had been the beloved daughter of Ethiopia's King, and now she was a slave to her father's enemy. She knew there was no hope of seeing Ethiopia again.

There was one source of light in her life, however. For Radames, the handsome young captain of the Egyptian Army, had fallen in love with the gentle, beautiful slave the moment he saw her. She, too, had fallen for Radames, despite his position as an enemy of her homeland.

They met often, in secret, by the Temple of Isis, and in the joy of their moments together, Radames confided his dreams to Aïda.

"I will lead the Egyptian Army to victory," he told her, "and when I return, our countries will be united, and you will become my bride and reign as the Queen of your people. It will not be long, I promise."

The day finally came when the Pharaoh was to hold court and announce the new leader of the war against Ethiopia.

Amid the majestic columns of a great hall in the palace, Egypt's High Priest, Ramfis, confided to Radames: "There are rumors that the Ethiopians plan to attack. Prepare yourself, for the Goddess Isis has chosen, and the great honor of leadership may be bestowed upon you."

All his life, Radames had dreamed of this day. If he became the new leader, he could return triumphant to free Aïda and marry her. "Ah, heavenly Aïda," he thought. "I could finally enthrone you in your native land."

Radames was deep in thought when Princess Amneris stepped from the shadows. She, too, was in love with the handsome leader, but she suspected he loved another.

Aïda suddenly appeared.

Oh, how Radames's eyes filled with passion! And when Amneris saw the look that passed between them, she was seized with suspicion and jealousy. Could Radames prefer a *slave* to the Princess of Egypt? It was intolerable! But her fury was interrupted by trumpets heralding the arrival of the Pharaoh.

A messenger came forward to give his report.

"Mighty Pharaoh, the Ethiopians have attacked. They are led by the fierce warrior King Amonasro, who has invaded Egypt!"

A thunder of anger broke out in court, and upon hearing her father's name, Aïda quietly cried out in fear.

The Pharaoh rose, and the crowd grew still.

"Radames will lead our army," he cried. "It is the decree of the Goddess Isis. Death to the Ethiopians! Victory to Egypt!" he shouted. "Return victorious, Radames!" he commanded.

"Return victorious! Return victorious!" the throng shouted, and Aïda, too, was stirred by the cry. In spite of herself, she also began to shout, "Return victorious! Return victorious!" as the court led the soldiers off to battle. Aïda was now left alone.

"Return victorious!" she called after Radames, but as her own voice echoed in the great hall, she suddenly realized she was asking for the death of her father, her mother, her friends, and all those she cherished. Yet how could she pray for the death of the man she loved?

Aïda was shocked. Her heart was torn between Radames and her loyalty to her father and Ethiopia. She fell to her knees and prayed.

"Oh, great gods of my youth!" she cried. "Pity me!"

That night, the halls of the temple rang as the priestesses chanted the sacred consecration song. The High Priest, Ramfis, led prayers to Phtha, the creator of life and mightiest Egyptian god, as he gave the great hero the sacred sword of Egypt.

"Let the sword of Radames be the strength of our nation! Let his bravery in battle crush the Ethiopians! Protect our land," they prayed, "and make Radames the most magnificent warrior of all."

"Praise to Phtha! Praise to Phtha!" the Egyptians chanted, and the priestesses danced a sacred dance to please the great god and ensure death to their enemies.

With Radames gone, time passed slowly for Aïda. But soon the prayers of the priests were granted. A special day dawned for Egypt—a day of ceremony and grandeur, of pomp and pageantry. The Ethiopians had been defeated at last.

Amneris sat before her mirror. Surrounded by slaves and adorned in her most beautiful gown and jewels, she was pleased with her reflection. Surely today when Radames returned, he would be struck by her radiance. Yet despite her vanity, she secretly burned with jealousy to think that Aïda, a mere handmaiden, might truly be loved by Radames.

So Amneris decided to test her privileged slave. And when gentle Aïda entered the royal chambers, Amneris sobbed, pretending great grief.

"Oh, Aïda, Aïda!" she cried in a shaking voice. "Egypt has lost its finest warrior. Radames has been killed in battle!"

Immediately Aïda wept with the pain of one whose heart has been broken forever. There was no longer any doubt in Amneris's mind.

"It is all a lie!" she shouted. "Radames was not killed. He lives!"

Aïda's tears of sorrow turned to tears of joy.

Overcome with fury, Amneris hurled Aïda to the floor. "How dare you, a lowly slave, love the same man loved by the Princess of Egypt?"

But Aïda, too, was a Princess. She rose proudly. She was about to tell Amneris the truth, but she stopped herself. Instead, with great difficulty, she asked to be forgiven.

"Have mercy on me," she begged. "Your power is unquestioned — you have all that a person could want. But what do I have to live for? My love of Radames, and that alone."

Aïda's plea only fueled Amneris's rage. She stormed out of the chamber, leaving Aïda to fear the worst.

Flags flew, and the entire city gathered to see the grand spectacle of the victory parade led by the Pharaoh, the Princess, and the High Priest. Trumpets blared, and dancing girls threw rose petals to form a welcoming carpet before the magnificent chariot of Radames.

The handsome warrior dismounted and knelt before the royal throne. When Amneris placed a laurel wreath on his head, the crowd was wild with joy.

"Hail to the conquerer!" they roared. "Hail to Radames!"

The Pharaoh proclaimed, "Radames, you are my greatest soldier. As a reward, whatever you wish shall be yours."

When Radames rose, he saw Aïda. Amneris saw the look of love on his face, and she was consumed with jealousy. Yet he dared not ask for Aïda's hand, not at that moment in public court.

"Mighty Pharaoh," he said instead, "I ask that you allow me to call forth our prisoners of war."

The Pharaoh granted Radames's request, and the Ethiopians were led into the square in chains. One tall, proud man stood out above the rest. Aïda gasped. It was her father!

The crowd was shocked to see her run and embrace him, but he whispered to her, "Do not betray that I am King."

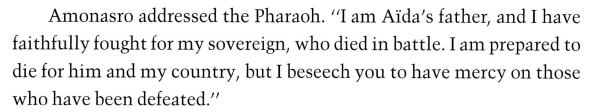

Amonasro addressed the Pharaoh. "I am Aïda's father, and I have faithfully fought for my sovereign, who died in battle. I am prepared to die for him and my country, but I beseech you to have mercy on those who have been defeated."

With outstretched arms, Aïda joined the Ethiopians. "Let the prisoners go free," she begged Radames and the Pharaoh.

So moved by her appeal, the Egyptian people joined in, and their cries urged the Pharaoh to allow the captured soldiers to be released.

"No!" the High Priest, Ramfis, cried. "The Ethiopians are still a threat and should be put to death."

"Their freedom is my wish," Radames told the Pharaoh.

"Unchain the Ethiopians!" the Pharaoh ordered. "But you, Aïda's father, must remain my prisoner as a pledge of your people's good faith."

An even greater reward was now to be bestowed upon Egypt's greatest warrior. The Pharaoh led Amneris to Radames.

"My daughter will be your bride," he proclaimed, joining their hands. "One day, you shall be Pharaoh, and together you will rule."

Radames was horrified. He dared not refuse the Pharaoh. He bowed and pretended gratitude, but his heart was filled with sorrow. Amneris looked scornfully at her handmaiden.

Aïda wept in her father's arms as the triumphant Egyptian Princess held Radames's hand and led him to the palace.

"Do not lose faith," Amonasro whispered to his daughter. "Ethiopia will soon avenge our conquerers."

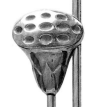

It was the eve of the great wedding, and a full moon shone on the dark waters of the River Nile beside the Temple of Isis. By boat, the High Priest, Ramfis, brought Amneris to the Temple. There she was to pray that her marriage be blessed. Little did she know that Radames had sent a message to Aïda, who was waiting to meet him nearby.

Aïda sadly watched the moonlit river and longed with all her heart and soul to return to her beloved homeland. Suddenly she heard Radames approach. But when the man came closer, she was stunned to see that it was her father, King Amonasro.

"Listen carefully, Aïda," he said sternly. "My plan will bring both you and Radames back to Ethiopia. Our soldiers stand ready to attack when I signal. There is a secret, unguarded road, but only Radames knows it. It is your duty as the Princess of Ethiopia to make him reveal this path."

"Father!" she cried, "I *cannot* betray Radames!"

With anger and disdain, King Amonasro forced her to her knees. "You are no longer my daughter! You are nothing more than a lowly slave of the Egyptians and a betrayer of your country! Have you forgotten your loved ones who were slaughtered without mercy by these, your enemies?"

"You are wrong! I am *not* and will *never* be a slave to anyone. I am the Princess of Ethiopia, and I have never forgotten my royal blood. My duty to you and to my country will always be first in my heart!"

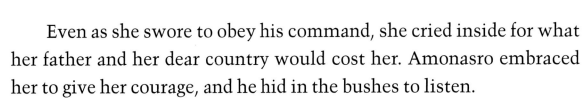

Even as she swore to obey his command, she cried inside for what her father and her dear country would cost her. Amonasro embraced her to give her courage, and he hid in the bushes to listen.

When Radames finally came, he was breathless with love. But Aïda turned on him scornfully.

"How could you betray me and marry Amneris as your reward?"

"Aïda, you have always been my love. My passion for you is deeper than the Nile, deeper than life itself," Radames told her.

"Then show me," Aïda demanded. "You have betrayed me. And if you truly love me, you will leave Egypt tonight and flee with me to Ethiopia. Only there will we find happiness and peace."

Radames was torn. The thought of leaving Egypt was unbearable, but the thought of living without Aïda was even more painful. At last, after much persuasion, he agreed to flee.

"The roads are heavily guarded by your soldiers. How will we escape?" she asked.

"All the roads are guarded except one," he told her. "The Gorges of Napata."

"The Gorges of Napata!" a voice rang out. Amonasro sprang from his hiding place. He was ready to attack with his army.

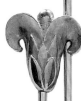
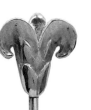

Radames could not believe it. "You, Aïda's father, are King of Ethiopia?" He was overcome. "I have sacrificed my country for my love of you!" he cried to Aïda.

"Come with us now," Amonasro told Radames. "You and Aïda will reign happily in Ethiopia."

But as the King took Radames's hand to lead him away, a shout rang out in the darkness. "Traitor!"

It was Amneris. She and the High Priest had come from the temple and had overheard the plot.

"Traitor!" she screamed again.

Amonasro leapt to kill Amneris with his dagger, but Radames ran between them to shield her.

"Go quickly!" he warned Aïda and Amonasro, and the King ran, dragging Aïda with him.

Radames stood before Amneris and the High Priest. He did not try to escape. Instead, he threw down his sword.

"I surrender!" he cried. "I am your prisoner!"

The treason of Radames shocked and infuriated all of Egypt. Guards locked him in the deepest dungeon in the palace. Soon his trial would begin, and he would be sentenced to a horrible death.

Amneris was in a state of grief. Her love for Radames had not diminished. Deep in her heart, she knew he had not meant to betray his country. Her own jealousy had made the mighty warrior a prisoner. She longed to beg her father, the Pharaoh, to release him, but she knew Radames still loved Aïda. She also knew soldiers had killed Amonasro, but Aïda had escaped and was still alive—somewhere.

In desperation, Amneris commanded the guards to bring Radames to her. She humbled herself and pleaded with him to forget Aïda.

"I will find a way to set you free, free to marry me and share the throne of Egypt," she said. "But you must never see Aïda again."

Radames refused. "You are Princess of Egypt, my country; and you have all that anyone could ask for. Yet I will always love Aïda, and there will never be room in my heart for anyone else."

The more Amneris begged him, the more strongly he refused.

When the priests came to take Radames, Amneris was in a rage of anger and jealousy, and she made no attempt to stop them. But when he left, she fell to the ground in tears, cringing as she heard the priests loudly accuse Radames of betrayal.

"Traitor! Traitor!" the High Priest, Ramfis, shouted again and again, but Radames never uttered a word to defend himself. Louder and louder the cruel accusations were hurled at him.

Amneris prayed to Isis and the other gods of Egypt to show mercy and save the man she loved, but the gods were silent.

The tribunal of priests pronounced Radames guilty of treason and sentenced him to be buried alive.

As the priests passed from the trial, Amneris flung herself before the High Priest. She insulted him and threatened revenge, but her cries were in vain.

"Radames, the traitor, will die," he said coldly.

Only the priests and guards were allowed to watch Radames walk into the deepest vault below. They sealed the last opening, shutting out all light and the last breath of fresh air. Alone, waiting quietly for death, Radames thought only of Aïda. He would never see her sparkling eyes and gentle smile again.

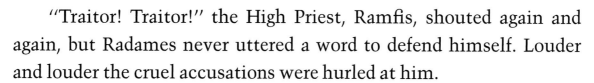

Suddenly, in the darkness, he heard Aïda's voice. At first, Radames thought it was a dream. But no—she had escaped and was hiding in the vault, waiting for him.

"Aïda, my love, you are too young and too beautiful to die."

Radames pushed in vain, trying to open the vault.

But Aïda gently placed her arms around him. With a tender kiss, she told him to stop.

"Remember, we will never be separated again. For eternity, we will be together."

And with all the love in the world, they held each other close—so close—as if they would never part.

Above their tomb, dressed in black, Princess Amneris prayed to the gods to forgive her and to grant heavenly rest to Radames, her love.

The gods granted her wish, but not as she hoped. For as she prayed to the gods and wept, a peaceful death had come to the Ethiopian Princess Aïda and Radames, the greatest warrior of Egypt. Finally they were together—forever in each other's arms.

STORYTELLER'S NOTE

Aïda as a heroine — and Aïda *as an opera — has been meaningful, poignant, and personal for me. In many ways, I believe Aïda is a portrait of my inner self.*

She was my best friend operatically and was a natural for me because my skin was my costume. This fact was a positive and strong feeling and allowed me a freedom of expression, of movement, and of interpretation that other operatic heroines I performed did not. I always felt, while performing Aïda, that I was expressing all of myself — as an American, as a woman, and as a human being.

Vocally, the role was perfectly suited to my voice in every respect — lyrically, dramatically, and in timbre. The role presented no difficulties, and because my voice was infused with the emotions I felt about Aïda, I sang with vocal ease and great enjoyment.

My first Grand Opera performance of this noble Ethiopian Princess's story was on the stage of the War Memorial Opera House in San Francisco in 1957. Totally prepared, eager, and excited, I performed my debut Aïda with great success. I went on to perform Aïda at the Chicago Lyric Opera House, the Arena di Verona and La Scala in Italy, the Vienna Staatsoper, the Paris Opera House, Covent Garden in London, the Hamburg Staatsoper in Germany, and my home opera house, the Metropolitan Opera House in New York City — where I performed the role more often than in any other opera house.

Aïda has given me great inspiration onstage and off. Her deep devotion and love for her country and for her people — her nobility, strength, and courage — are all qualities I aspire to as a human being. I will never forget her.

— Leontyne Price